What
Is a
Food Web?

Grassland
Food Webs
in Action

Paul Fleisher

Lerner Publications Company
Minneapolis

Lerner Publications Company
A division of Lerner Publishing Group, Inc.
241 First Avenue North
Minneapolis, MN 55401 U.S.A.

Website address: www.lernerbooks.com

Library of Congress Cataloging-in-Publication Data

Fleisher, Paul.
    Grassland food webs in action / by Paul Fleisher.
        p.   cm. — (Searchlight books™—what is a food web?)
    Includes index.
    ISBN 978-1-4677-1293-4 (lib. bdg. : alk. paper)
    ISBN 978-1-4677-1775-5 (eBook)
    1. Grassland ecology—Juvenile literature. 2. Grassland plants—Juvenile literature.
    3. Grassland animals—Juvenile literature. I. Title.
    QH541.5.P7F58 2014
    577.4—dc23   2012032548

Manufactured in the United States of America
1 – BP – 7/15/13

Contents

A GRASSLAND FOOD WEB

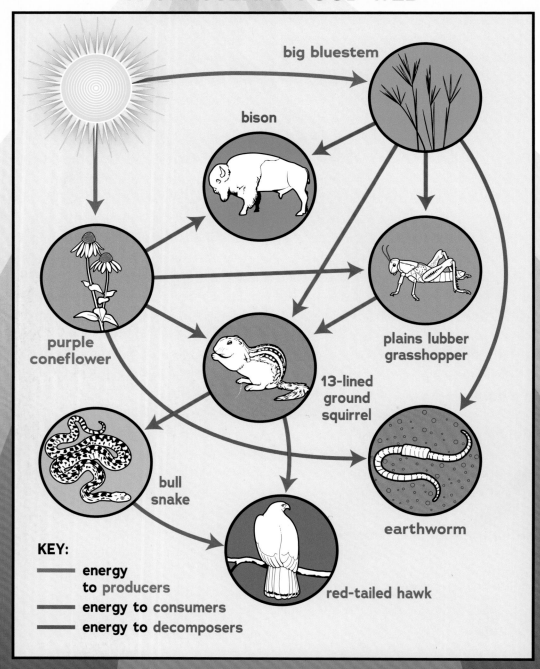

big bluestem

bison

purple
coneflower

plains lubber
grasshopper

13-lined
ground
squirrel

bull
snake

earthworm

red-tailed hawk

KEY:
energy
to producers
energy to consumers
energy to decomposers

Chapter 1

GRASSLANDS

Tall grasses bend in the wind.
Insects buzz in the warm air.
Birds soar through the clear blue
sky. There are few trees. You can see
for miles. You are in a grassland.

This place is a grassland. What are some things you might see in a grassland?

Grasslands are found in many parts of the world. In the United States and Canada, grasslands are called prairies. In other places, they are called steppes or savannas.

Grasslands are found in places that don't get enough rain for many large trees to grow. Instead, grasses and other low plants grow there. These plants need less water than big trees.

In Africa, grasslands are called savannas. Savannas have only a few trees.

Important Environments

Grasslands are some of Earth's most important environments. An environment is the place where any creature lives. The environment includes air, soil, weather, and other plants and animals.

Pronghorn antelopes eat grasses and other plants.

Foxes eat meat. This fox is eating a pheasant.

Plants and animals in a grassland depend on one another. Some animals eat plants. Some animals are meat eaters. They eat other animals. When plants and animals die, they break down into chemicals. The chemicals become part of the soil. Some of these chemicals help plants grow.

Food Chains

Energy moves from one living thing to another. A food chain shows how the energy moves. The energy for life comes from the sun. Plants store the sun's energy in their leaves, stems, and roots. When an animal eats a plant, the animal gets some of the sun's energy from the plant. The energy moves farther along the food chain each time one living thing eats another.

A lion is hunting a zebra. If the lion eats the zebra, the lion will get energy from the zebra.

Grasslands have many food chains. Imagine that a prairie dog eats some grass. Then a hawk eats the prairie dog. When the hawk dies, a vulture eats its body. The sun's energy passes from the grass to the prairie dog. Then it goes to the hawk. Then it passes to the vulture.

This prairie dog is eating grass.

Food Webs

But prairie dogs don't eat only grass. They eat many different kinds of plants. Hawks eat other animals besides prairie dogs. They also eat mice and small birds. And vultures eat all kinds of dead animals. An environment's food web is made of many food chains. A food web shows how all creatures depend on one another for food.

This red-tailed hawk is eating a mouse.

Chapter 2

GRASSLAND PLANTS

Plants use sunlight to make food. Because plants produce food, they are called producers. Plants also make oxygen. Oxygen is a gas in the air. The way plants make food and oxygen is called photosynthesis. Plants need carbon dioxide, sunlight, and water for photosynthesis. Carbon dioxide is another gas in the air.

A grassland's energy comes from the sun. Plants use sunlight to make food. What else do plants make?

A plant's leaves take in carbon dioxide and sunlight. The plant's roots take in water. The plant uses energy from sunlight to turn the carbon dioxide and water into sugar and starch. Sugar and starch are the plant's own food. The plant stores this food in its leaves and roots.

HOW PHOTOSYNTHESIS WORKS

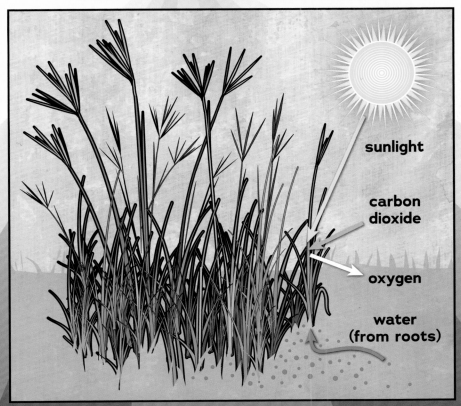

sunlight

carbon dioxide

oxygen

water (from roots)

The leaves of big bluestem grass turn sunlight, carbon dioxide, and water into food for the plant.

As the plant makes food, it also makes oxygen. The oxygen goes into the air. Animals breathe in the oxygen. They breathe out carbon dioxide. Plants use the carbon dioxide to make more food.

ALL ANIMALS BREATHE OXYGEN. THESE ANIMALS ARE GUANACOS. THEY LIVE IN GRASSLANDS IN SOUTH AMERICA.

Nutrients

Plants grow in soil. The soil contains special chemicals called nutrients. Living things need nutrients to grow. When it rains, water soaks into the soil. Nutrients from the soil go into the water. When a plant's roots take in the water, the plant gets nutrients from the soil too. The nutrients become part of the plant.

Soil has nutrients that plants need to grow.

The Most Important Plants

Grasses are the most important plants in a grassland. Many different grasses grow on the prairie. Big bluestem, Indian grass, and switchgrass are prairie grasses.

Some prairie grasses grow up to 9 feet (3 meters) tall. That's taller than a basketball player!

Prairie grasses have long roots. The roots grow deep into the ground. The roots hold the soil in place. They keep the soil from being blown away or washed away by rain.

When the prairie gets very dry, the leaves of the grasses die. But under the ground, the roots stay alive. When it rains, new leaves grow from the roots.

Grass plants have long roots. The roots are usually longer than the plant is tall.

Other Plants

Other plants grow on prairies too. Wildflowers grow among the grasses. Sunflowers, coneflowers, clover, and daisies grow there.

The prairie has some bushes and small trees too. Chokecherry, wild plum, crab apple, and prairie rose grow on the prairie. Sagebrush grows in drier parts of the prairie.

Many different kinds of wildflowers grow on the prairie.

A few larger trees grow on the prairie. They grow near streams or ponds. In these places, trees can get enough water to grow. Cottonwood, walnut, hackberry, and maple trees grow on the prairie.

Cottonwood trees are growing along the banks of this river.

Chapter 3

GRASSLAND PLANT EATERS

Animals are called consumers. *Consume* means "eat." Animals that eat plants are called herbivores. The sun's energy is stored inside plants. When an animal eats a plant, the animal gets the sun's energy.

Zebras and gazelles are plant eaters that live in Africa. What are some other animals that eat plants?

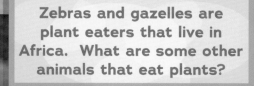

Insects

Many insects are herbivores. Caterpillars, grasshoppers, and leafhoppers eat grasses and other plants. Butterflies, moths, and bees drink nectar. Nectar is a sweet liquid flowers make.

GRASSHOPPERS EAT GRASSES AND OTHER KINDS OF PLANTS.

Pheasants eat plant seeds, berries, and insects.

Birds

Many grassland birds eat plant seeds. Goldfinches crack seeds in their beaks. Sparrows and pheasants eat seeds too.

Mammals

Prairie dogs, rabbits, and pocket gophers are also herbivores. They live in holes in the ground. Living underground helps these animals stay safe. When they are underground, it is harder for meat eaters to find and eat them.

Bison live on the prairie too. They move from place to place, eating prairie grasses. Pronghorn antelopes also eat prairie grasses.

Pocket gophers live in holes in the ground. They eat plant roots, grasses, and seeds.

Chapter 4

GRASSLAND MEAT EATERS

Some grassland animals eat meat. These animals are called carnivores. Carnivores eat animals. But they need plants too. Carnivores get energy by eating animals that have eaten plants.

Prairie rattlesnakes eat meat. What do we call animals that eat meat?

Spiders and Wasps

Spiders are carnivores. Some spiders weave sticky webs. They use the webs to catch insects to eat. Wasps hunt insects too. They feed the insects to their babies.

The crab spider sitting on this flower has caught a fly to eat.

Birds

Many birds eat insects. Cowbirds follow big animals such as bison. When bison walk, they scare insects. The insects fly away from the bison. Then cowbirds catch the insects. Bluebirds and red-winged blackbirds eat insects too.

Other kinds of birds are also carnivores. Kestrels eat small birds. Red-tailed hawks fly high above the prairie. They hunt birds, snakes, and lizards.

A cowbird is sitting on this bison's back.

Snakes and Mammals

Milk snakes eat small animals. They hunt mice, rats, pocket gophers, lizards, other snakes, and birds. They also eat bird eggs.

Foxes eat mostly meat. They hunt mice, rabbits, pocket gophers, and prairie dogs. They eat birds and snakes too.

This milk snake is eating a rat.

Weasels and ferrets are long and thin. They can crawl into the underground holes where small animals live. Weasels and ferrets hunt prairie dogs, gophers, mice, and rats.

FERRETS HAVE LONG, NARROW BODIES.

Omnivores

Some animals eat both plants and meat. These animals are called omnivores. Box turtles are omnivores. They eat leaves, fruit, snails, worms, insects, and bird eggs. Coyotes are omnivores too. Coyotes hunt small animals. They also eat bird eggs and fruit.

This coyote is hunting for mice.

Chapter 5

GRASSLAND DECOMPOSERS

All living things die. When plants and animals die, they decay. They break down into nutrients. Living things called decomposers help dead things decay. Decomposers feed on dead plants and animals.

These are the bones of a deer. The rest of the deer's body has been eaten away. What do we call living things that feed on dead animals?

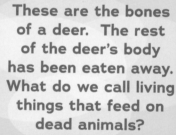

Decomposers are nature's recyclers. They break down dead plants and animals. Nutrients from the dead plants and animals go into the soil. Then other living things can use the nutrients.

Decomposers are very important. Without them, grasslands would be full of dead plants and animals. Then no new plants could grow. Animals would run out of food.

Earthworms eat dead plants. They break the plants down into nutrients.

Bacteria and Fungi

The prairie's most important decomposers live in soil.
Bacteria are tiny living things. They are much too small
to see. Millions of them live in soil. Mushrooms and
other fungi live in soil too. Bacteria and fungi feed on
dead plants and animals.

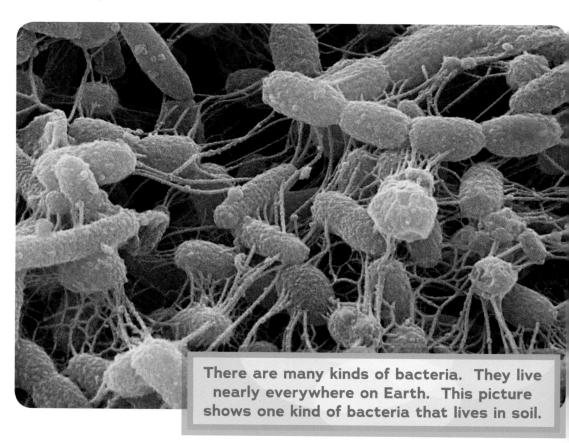

There are many kinds of bacteria. They live
nearly everywhere on Earth. This picture
shows one kind of bacteria that lives in soil.

Worms and Insects

Earthworms burrow into the soil. They eat bits of dead leaves. Some insects lay eggs in rotting wood. Young insects hatch from the eggs. The young insects eat the wood.

When an animal dies, insects lay their eggs in its body. The young insects feed on the animal's body.

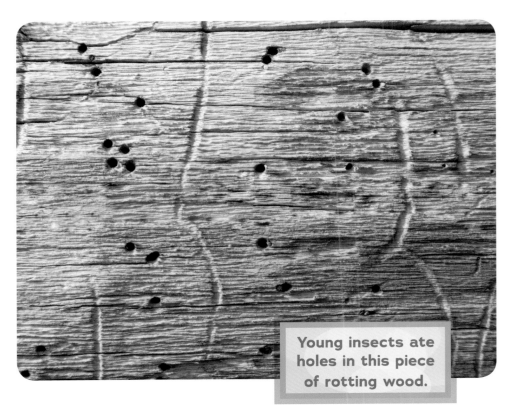

Young insects ate holes in this piece of rotting wood.

Chapter 6

PEOPLE AND GRASSLANDS

Grasslands are important to people. Many people live on the prairie. They live in towns and cities.

The prairie is a good place for cattle to live. The cattle eat prairie grasses. People raise cattle to get beef to eat and milk to drink. Beef is meat that comes from cattle.

These cattle are eating grass. Why do people raise cattle?

Prairie soil is good for growing crops. Farmers grow wheat and corn on the prairie. People need these crops for food. Usually farmers plow the ground before they plant crops. Plowing breaks up soil so crops can be planted in rows.

But plowing can harm grasslands. Plowing cuts the roots of prairie plants. The roots no longer hold soil in place. Wind can blow soil away. Rain can wash it away. Without soil, plants can't grow.

This farmer is plowing the ground to plant crops.

Protecting Grasslands

Farmers can plant some crops without plowing. That way, the roots of dead plants stay in the ground. They hold the soil in place. Planting trees along the edges of fields protects the soil too. The trees block some of the wind. That helps keep the soil from blowing away.

Trees are growing around these farm fields. The trees help to keep the soil from blowing away.

Other people can protect some grasslands by making them into parks. In these parks, no one plows the ground. No one mows the grasses. Wild plants and animals can live in the parks. Prairie grasses can grow deep roots.

Some places in the United States have prairie parks. Other parts of the world have grassland parks too. It's important to help grasslands thrive as they did long ago.

OSAGE PRAIRIE IS A GRASSLAND PARK IN MISSOURI.

Glossary

bacteria: tiny living things that are made up of just one cell. Bacteria can be seen only under a microscope.

carnivore: an animal that eats meat

consumer: a living thing that eats other living things

decay: to break down

decomposer: a living thing that feeds on dead plants and animals

environment: a place where creatures live. An environment includes the air, soil, weather, plants, and animals in a place.

food chain: the way energy moves from the sun to a plant, then to a plant eater, then to a meat eater, and finally to a decomposer

food web: many food chains connected together. A food web shows how all living things in a place need one another for food.

herbivore: an animal that eats only plants

nutrient: a chemical that living things need in order to grow

omnivore: an animal that eats both plants and meat

oxygen: a gas in the air. All animals need oxygen to breathe.

photosynthesis: the way green plants use energy from sunlight to make their own food out of carbon dioxide and water

prairie: a grassland in the United States and Canada

producer: a living thing that makes its own food

Learn More about Grasslands and Food Webs

Books

Johnson, Rebecca L. *A Walk in the Prairie*. Minneapolis: Lerner Publications Company, 2001. This book takes readers on a walk through the prairie and illustrates how each living creature is part of a circle of life.

Wojahn, Rebecca Hogue, and Donald Wojahn. *A Savanna Food Chain: A Who-Eats-What Adventure in Africa*. Minneapolis: Lerner Publications Company, 2009. What you choose to eat shapes your fate in this fun interactive story about food chains.

Zoehfeld, Kathleen Weidner. *Secrets of the Garden: Food Chains and the Food Web in Our Backyard*. New York: Alfred A. Knopf, 2012. This book takes a fun approach to examining food chains and the food web that exist in one family's backyard garden.

Websites

Biomes of the World: Grasslands
http://www.mbgnet.net/sets/grasslnd/?b467e680
This website includes photos of many plants and animals that live in grasslands around the world.

Chain Reaction
http://www.ecokids.ca/pub/eco_info/topics/frogs/chain_reaction
Create a food chain and find out what happens if one link is taken out of the chain.

Food Chains and Webs
http://www.vtaide.com/png/foodchains.htm
This website has an interactive tool to let you create your own food webs.

Grassland Animal Printouts
http://www.enchantedlearning.com/biomes/grassland/grassland.shtml
This page has links to information about many kinds of animals that live in grasslands around the world.

Index

Photo Acknowledgments

The images in this book are used with the permission of: © Zeke Smith/Independent Service, pp. 4, 13; Bureau of Land Management, p. 5; © Alextara/Dreamstime.com, p. 6; © iStock.com/ Dennis Donohue, p. 7; © NHPA/SuperStock, p. 8; © David Youldon/Dreamstime.com, p. 9; © iStock.com/Sascha Burkard, p. 10; © Oldclimber/Dreamstime.com, p. 11; © Aliaksandr Mazurkevich/Dreamstime.com, p. 12; © John R. Kreul/Independent Picture Service, p. 14; © iStockphoto. com/mycola, p. 15; © iStockphoto.com/Weldon Schloneger, p. 16; © iStockphoto.com/redmal, p. 17; © IStockphoto.com/Steve Geer, p. 18; © iStockphoto.com/Denice Breaux, p. 19; © Sekernas/ Dreamstime.com, p. 20; © iStockphoto.com/Ralph Loesche, p. 21; Photo courtesy of USDA Natural Resources Conservation Service, pp. 22, 36; © South12th/Dreamstime.com, p. 23; © iStockphoto. com/David Parsons, p. 24; © Brian Lasenby/Dreamstime.com, p. 25; © Julie Lubick/Dreamstime. com, p. 26; © Michael & Patricia Fogden/Minden Pictures, p. 27; Ryan Hagerty/U.S. Fish and Wildlife Service, p. 28; © iStockphoto.com/Frank Leung, p. 29; © iStockphoto.com/Terry North, p. 30; © photofun/Shutterstock.com, p. 31; © David Scharf/Science Faction/SuperStock, p. 32; © pzAxe/ Shutterstock.com, p. 33; © Lorraine Swanson/Dreamstime.com, p. 34; © iStockphoto.com/Dušan Kostić, p. 35; © Richard Thom/Visuals Unlimited, Inc., p. 37.
Front Cover: © altrendo nature/Altrendo/Getty Images

Main body text set in Adrianna Regular 14/20
Typeface provided by Chank